The Unseen Edges: 20 Secrets to Compound Business Success

Pen Tillman & Ally Forsyth

Published by

Pen Tillman

Deckademy Pty Ltd

tillmanforsythpublishings@gmail.com

v.1.0.04

This page is intentionally left blank.

<u>**Foreword**</u>

The Unseen Edges: 20 Secrets to Compound Business Success

This book exists because the loudest voices in business rarely tell the full story.

Most advice glorifies speed, spectacle, and scale at any cost: the overnight unicorn, the viral launch, the 100-hour weeks that supposedly forge empires. It sells drama and instant gratification. Yet the companies and founders that quietly endure—and eventually dominate—are rarely built that way.

They are built on edges most people never notice, never defend, and never compound long enough to see the result.

The principles in these pages are not revolutionary in the headline sense. They do not promise shortcuts or overnight transformation. They are structural, often uncomfortable, and deliberately quiet:

- Choosing signal over noise when everything screams for attention
- Distributing real ownership gravity instead of symbolic equity
- Imposing elegant constraint when abundance feels safer
- Prioritising decision velocity over endless consensus
- Mastering boring excellence while others chase flashy innovation
- Thinking in decades when the world demands quarters

These are not sexy. They do not trend on social feeds. They do not make for compelling pitch-deck slides. But they compound—slowly, relentlessly, unfairly.

The authors of this book are based in Sydney, where the startup ecosystem sits at the edge of the world—geographically distant from Silicon Valley yet deeply connected to global markets, APAC opportunities, and the unique pressures of building in a high-cost, lifestyle-conscious environment. From this vantage point, the difference between short-term flash and long-term endurance becomes especially clear. Capital is disciplined here. Imitation arrives fast. Attention is hard-won. The quiet compounding edges matter more than ever.

In 2026, the landscape has shifted again. Capital flows are more disciplined. Imitation happens in days, not months. AI agents handle tasks that once required teams. Attention is more fractured than ever. Yet the separation between good outcomes and legendary ones still comes down to the same thing: who is willing to consistently choose and protect the unseen edges when no one is watching.

This is not a formula to follow blindly. It is a set of currents—principles you can choose to enter or ignore. Step into one for ninety days. Feel the initial resistance. Then feel the momentum as small refusals and small obsessions begin to pull the trajectory in a new direction. Add the next current when the first has become instinct.

The water is deeper than it appears. The edges are sharper than they look. And the compounding is more powerful than almost anyone realises.

If you are here because you want to build something that lasts—something that survives hype cycles, funding winters, copycats, and your own fatigue—then these pages are for you.

Swim deliberately.
The long game rewards the quiet.

— The Team
March 2026

Chapter 1: The First Secret – Obsess Over Signal-to-Noise Ratio

In the fast-moving world of 2026, the single biggest edge isn't more intelligence, more money, or even more talent—it's clarity. The highest-performing founders and leaders don't possess more information than everyone else. They possess far less *irrelevant* information. They maintain an exceptionally high signal-to-noise ratio (SNR).

Borrowed from engineering, signal is the valuable, predictive data you need—the clear voice in a call, the reliable pattern in chaos. Noise is everything that interferes: static, distractions, low-value inputs. In business, your daily flood includes emails, notifications, social media trends, competitor rumours, economic headlines, team side conversations, vanity metrics, and endless "urgent" requests. The vast majority is noise. Only a small fraction is true signal: inputs that reliably forecast outcomes or unlock high-leverage actions.

Kevin O'Leary, the Shark Tank investor, has shared what he observed from working with Steve Jobs in the early 1990s. Jobs operated with an intense focus he described as an 80/20 signal-to-noise ratio: roughly 80% of his energy went to signal (the 3–5 truly critical tasks he needed to complete in his next 18 waking hours), and only 20% to everything else, which he treated as noise. Anything that didn't advance those priorities— random requests, distractions, low-impact meetings—was ruthlessly filtered out. O'Leary has contrasted this with Elon Musk, whom he describes as pushing toward 100% signal, zero noise. Musk has been known to walk away mid-conversation the instant he detects no useful information flowing, unwilling to tolerate even minimal waste.

These aren't personality quirks. They're deliberate systems for preserving mental bandwidth in a world designed to fragment it. Most entrepreneurs run the opposite ratio: 20% signal drowned in 80% noise. They react to every alert, chase every shiny trend, and wonder why real progress feels exhausting despite endless activity.

 Why Signal-to-Noise Is the Foundational Secret

Clarity underpins everything else:
- Ruthless prioritization becomes possible only when you can identify real signal.
- Fast, confident decisions emerge when you're not paralysed by conflicting inputs.
- Strong culture and execution scale when the leader isn't constantly derailed.

High-SNR operators often seem "intuitive" or "lucky." In truth, they notice and act on faint but genuine signals while others are overwhelmed. That small, consistent advantage compounds into massive separation over time.

How to Build and Defend Your Own High Signal-to-Noise Ratio

Here are concrete, proven ways to raise your SNR—start implementing one today.

1. Create Your Personal Signal Dashboard (Limit to 3–5 Metrics)
Resist the temptation of 20+ KPIs. Choose only 3–5 true leading indicators that have historically predicted most of your major wins and losses. These should be forward-looking, not lagging vanity stats (total revenue this month, follower count).

2026-relevant examples by business type:

- SaaS/Subscription: Weekly active users as % of total, first-session "aha" moment completion rate, early churn signals (usage drop in weeks 2–4), customer effort score from support.
- E-commerce/DTC: 30-day repeat purchase rate, mobile add-to-cart-to-purchase conversion trend, customer acquisition payback period shortening.
- Marketplace platforms: New supplier/seller retention velocity (e.g., listing 3+ times in first month), cross-side engagement (messages per active pair), cohort liquidity speed.
- B2B services: Net promoter score trend in first 90 days, scope-expansion rate among clients, referral velocity per active client.

Quick exercise: List your last 5 big successes and 5 big failures. What early indicators appeared in the wins but were absent or weak in the losses? Those become your dashboard. Review weekly—never daily—to avoid noise creep.

2. Apply the "Noise Tax" Rule

Force every new input to justify itself. Before starting a new tool, channel, meeting, conference, mastermind, or even casual coffee chat, write one clear paragraph:

- Which of my 3–5 dashboard metrics will this realistically move?
- In what direction, and by roughly how much?
- What's the worst credible downside?

No clear, honest answer? Decline. This single filter can eliminate 60–80% of incoming distractions.

3. Run a Quarterly "Kill List" Ritual

Every 90 days, list every active project, channel, tool, recurring meeting, report, or experiment. Score each: Has it meaningfully advanced a signal metric in the past quarter? (Yes/No)

Anything with three straight "No" scores gets permanently cut—no grandfathering. The discomfort is intentional; it retrains your system to prize clarity over completion or comfort.

4. Protect Cognitive Peak Hours & Energy

Most people think clearest in the morning. Guard those hours:

- No meetings before 11 a.m. unless it's a rare Type 1 (irreversible) decision.

- Batch low-signal tasks (email, admin, social scrolling) into 1–2 focused windows.

- Use deep-work rituals: 90-minute blocks, phone in another room, noise-cancelling headphones with instrumental audio.

- End each day with a 5-minute audit: "What actually moved my dashboard today? What was pure noise?"

The Long-Term Compounding Effect

Founders who master SNR don't just work more efficiently—they perceive farther ahead. They spot subtle shifts (a 6% week-over-week lift in activation rate) and act while others debate headlines. They hire better by ignoring resume buzzwords and focusing on real signal. They pivot decisively because noise doesn't cloud judgment.

Over quarters and years, the advantage turns exponential.

Start tonight: Define your 3–5 dashboard metrics. Tomorrow, enforce the Noise Tax on your next incoming request. Block your first Kill List review for the end of this quarter.

Clarity isn't accidental. It's engineered—and defended—every day.

Chapter 2: The Ownership Illusion

Most founders believe they "own" the business because their name is on the shares, the cap table shows a large percentage, and the headaches land squarely on their desk. But legal ownership is only part of the story. The real power—and the real secret to scaling sustainably—lies in psychological ownership: the deep, intrinsic feeling that "this is mine to protect, grow, and improve." When that feeling exists only at the top, the company stays small, fragile, and dependent on one person's energy. When it spreads wide and deep, extraordinary things happen: initiative explodes, loyalty deepens, and the business begins to run itself in the best possible way.

This is the ownership illusion. Founders often think granting equity or bonuses creates alignment. Sometimes it does. More often, it creates paper owners who still act like employees—clocking in, doing the minimum, waiting for direction. True ownership gravity pulls people in because they feel emotionally invested, not just financially.

Research backs this powerfully. Studies on employee-owned companies (via ESOPs, broad equity grants, or co-ops) show that psychological ownership—not just legal shares—mediates the biggest gains in commitment, voice behaviour (speaking up with ideas), helping behaviour, and overall performance. When employees feel like genuine stewards of the business, they innovate more, stay longer, defend the company fiercely, and deliver higher productivity. One meta-analysis and multiple longitudinal studies confirm: legal ownership alone is weak; it's the sense of "this is mine" that drives outsized results.

Real-world examples illustrate the payoff:

- WinCo Foods (employee-owned grocery chain): Frontline workers like cashiers and stockers became millionaires through compounded equity growth. One long-time employee reported nearly $1 million in stock value—enough to retire early. The company attributes low turnover and relentless efficiency to this widespread ownership mindset.
- C.H.I. Overhead Doors (under KKR ownership): Every employee, from factory floor to truck drivers, received equity stakes. When sold, payouts averaged $175,000+ per person (some much higher), with long-timers receiving up to $800,000. Workers described a "culture of ownership" that transformed daily effort.
- SRC (Springfield ReManufacturing Corp.): After a leveraged buyout, the company shared ownership broadly. It created dozens of blue-collar millionaires and paid out over $100 million to retiring employee-owners, all while sustaining high performance through radical transparency.

These aren't rare unicorns. Broad-based equity programs at companies like Bank of America (awarding $1B+ in stock to non-executives in recent years) and initiatives from private equity firms (Ownership Works, Blackstone, etc.) show the pattern: when frontline people feel real skin in the game, engagement and results compound.

The Secret in Action: Create Ownership Gravity

Distribute real ownership—financial and psychological—far wider than feels comfortable. Here's how to do it without diluting yourself into irrelevance.

1. Give Equity-Like Incentives to Frontline Touchpoints

Not just execs and early engineers—extend meaningful stakes to customer-facing roles, support teams, ops leads, and key individual contributors.

- Use restricted stock units (RSUs), profit interests, phantom equity, or revenue-share pools tied to milestones.

- Target: Aim for 10–20% of total equity pool allocated to non-leadership over time (broad-based plans often succeed with 5–15% grants).

- Example: In SaaS, give support reps equity vesting based on customer retention metrics they influence directly.

2. Run Quarterly "Ownership Audits"

Ask brutally honest questions about every key person:

- Does this individual behave like an owner today? (Proactive ideas, protects resources, fights for the mission even when inconvenient?)

- Would I fight to keep them if a competitor tried to poach?

Score on a simple 1–10 scale. Top scorers get disproportionate rewards (bonus equity, promotions, public recognition). Bottom scorers get coaching—or gentle exit paths.

This isn't annual performance review theatre; it's a living filter that reinforces owner-like behaviour.

3. Celebrate "Owner Moments" Publicly and Frequently

Spotlight real examples of ownership in action:

- A developer who fixed a systemic bug on their weekend without being asked.

- A sales rep who turned down a big deal because it would hurt long-term customer trust.

- An ops person who redesigned a process saving $50k/year.

Use company-wide shoutouts, small equity bonuses, or "owner rings" (symbolic but meaningful tokens). Repetition builds culture: people see what gets rewarded and emulate it.

4. Tie Ownership to Transparency and Influence

Psychological ownership grows when people have:

- Intimate knowledge → Share open books monthly (revenue, margins, key metrics).

- Control/influence → Give frontline teams real decision rights in their domain (e.g., customer support can approve refunds up to $X without approval).

- Extended control → Long vesting periods (4–5 years) so people feel invested over time.

Research shows these three pathways (knowledge, control, investment) are the strongest predictors of feeling like an owner.

Companies with high psychological ownership don't just retain talent—they attract it. Top performers seek environments where their efforts directly shape outcomes and rewards. In Sydney's competitive startup scene (fintech, SaaS, healthtech hubs), this edge is massive: talent wars are won by founders who make people feel like co-owners, not hired hands.

The illusion breaks when the founder realizes: you don't scale a business by hoarding ownership—you scale it by multiplying owners. Do this right, and the weight lifts. The business starts pulling you forward instead of you dragging it.

Action steps for today:
- List your top 10 non-executive contributors. Which already act like owners?
- Draft a simple frontline equity experiment (even 0.5–1% pool for key roles).
- Schedule your first ownership audit for next quarter.

Ownership isn't divided—it's multiplied. Spread it wisely, and watch gravity do the work.

Chapter 3: The Power of Elegant Constraint

Abundance is the silent killer of more businesses than scarcity ever was. Unlimited budget, endless features, infinite team size, no hard deadlines—these sound like freedom, but they breed mediocrity, bloat, and distraction. When resources feel infinite, decisions become lazy, innovation stalls, and excellence gets diluted in a sea of "good enough."

The counter-intuitive truth: elegant constraint—deliberately imposing smart, artificial limits—forces clarity, creativity, and breakthrough results. Constraints don't handcuff genius; they channel it. As Antoine de Saint-Exupéry famously wrote in *Terre des Hommes* (Wind, Sand and Stars): "Perfection is achieved, not when there is nothing more to add, but when there is nothing left to take away." This principle, rooted in design and engineering, applies powerfully to business. Removing the unnecessary sharpens what remains.

Real-world evidence supports this. A comprehensive review of 145 empirical studies found that moderate constraints stimulate novel thinking and creativity—only excessive ones stifle it. Companies facing resource scarcity often birth innovative models: Airbnb and Uber emerged during the 2008 recession by creatively recombining underused assets (homes, cars) under economic pressure. Toyota's just-in-time manufacturing arose from post-war Japan's severe resource limits, forcing elegant efficiency that later became a global standard.

Steve Jobs exemplified this at Apple in the late 1990s. Facing near-bankruptcy, he slashed the product lineup from dozens to a handful of focused items (iMac, iPod path). By ruthlessly constraining options, Apple avoided dilution and poured energy into what mattered—leading to one of the greatest turnarounds in corporate history.

In modern contexts, startups in emerging markets or underfunded teams frequently outperform resource-rich incumbents through "bricolage"—making do with what's at hand in creative combinations. Selective bricolage (targeted, disciplined use of constraints) expands competitiveness, while unchecked abundance leads to "tinkering traps" and second-best compromises.

Why Constraints Breed Elegance

- They force prioritization: With limited resources, you must ruthlessly choose what truly creates value.
- They spark creativity: Necessity eliminates lazy "add more" thinking and pushes for smarter, simpler solutions.
- They prevent bloat: Unlimited options invite feature creep, scope creep, and cultural drift.
- They accelerate learning: Tight constraints shorten feedback loops—fail fast, iterate elegantly.

Without constraints, teams chase shiny objects. With them, they build something refined and defensible.

How to Engineer Elegant Constraint in Your Business

Implement these practical, battle-tested constraints—start with one or two immediately.

1. The "One Metric per Department per Quarter" Rule

Each team (product, marketing, sales, ops, support) gets exactly one primary metric to own and move for the quarter. No more.

- Product: e.g., activation rate (users reaching core value in first session).
- Marketing: e.g., qualified lead velocity (not total leads).
- Sales: e.g., win rate on qualified pipeline.

Everything else becomes secondary or experimental. This forces laser focus—departments stop diffusing energy across 10 vanity goals.

Pro tip: At quarter-end, celebrate only movement on that one metric. The rest gets acknowledged quietly or ignored.

2. 72-Hour Feature Freeze Post-Launch

After releasing any feature, product, or update: no changes for 72 hours. No bug fixes (unless critical), no tweaks, no additions.

Why? Immediate post-launch is peak observation time—real user behaviour emerges before you "fix" what isn't broken. This constraint forces better upfront design and deeper learning from actual usage. Many teams discover the "real" problem only after resisting the urge to fiddle.

3. The Anti-Growth Budget (10–15% Defense Allocation)

When planning for aggressive growth, proactively allocate 10–15% of resources to defend against success. Ask:

- If revenue doubles in 12 months, what breaks first? (Support volume, margins, culture, ops capacity?)

- If team size triples, how do we avoid losing our edge?

Fund experiments, systems, hiring buffers, or culture rituals to protect core strengths. This turns growth from a threat into a controlled advantage. Companies that ignore this often scale into chaos.

4. The "No New Initiatives" Sprint (90-Day Blackout Periods)

Every 6–9 months, declare a 90-day window where no new projects, channels, tools, or experiments start—only finishing, killing, or optimizing existing ones.

This kills shiny-object syndrome, surfaces hidden waste, and forces teams to extract maximum value from what's already built. The relief is palpable; momentum returns.

5. Personal Constraint Rituals for Founders

- Cap your direct reports at 5–7 (forces delegation and talent density).

- Limit strategic meetings to 60 minutes max, with one decision owner.

- Enforce "no-meeting Wednesdays" or mornings for deep work.

These self-imposed limits protect your own signal-to-noise (tying back to Chapter 1) and model disciplined behaviour.

The Compounding Payoff

Teams operating under elegant constraints don't just survive—they thrive with sharper products, happier cultures, and stronger unit economics. In

Sydney's competitive ecosystem—where capital is plentiful but attention and talent are scarce—these principles give you an unfair edge. Founders who embrace constraint appear disciplined and visionary; those who chase abundance often burn out or bloat into irrelevance.

Start small: Pick one constraint this week (e.g., one-metric rule for your key team). Feel the initial resistance—that friction is creativity knocking. Lean into it.

Abundance is comfortable. Constraint is elegant. Choose elegance.

Chapter 4: Decision Velocity – The Invisible Moat

In a world accelerating toward AI-driven everything, traditional moats like patents, brand loyalty, and network effects still matter—but they're eroding faster than ever. The new, often invisible moat that separates winners from the pack in 2026 is decision velocity: the speed and quality with which an organization identifies, debates, decides, and acts on opportunities or threats.

Speed alone isn't enough—it's speed with learning. Companies that move fast without learning generate motion, not progress. Those that learn fast and act fast compound advantages rapidly. Recent analyses highlight this shift: decision velocity is emerging as the defining competitive edge in AI-infused markets, where data abundance meets uncertainty. Leaders who reduce decision cycle time while maintaining high quality capture market share, pricing power, and talent before slower rivals even finish debating.

Amazon's Jeff Bezos codified this years ago in his shareholder letters: most decisions should be made with ~70% of the desired information. Waiting for 90% often means being too slow. He emphasized high-velocity decisions through frameworks like classifying choices as irreversible ("one-way doors," deliberate and slow) vs. reversible ("two-way doors," fast and lightweight). This bias for action—combined with mechanisms to preserve quality—has powered Amazon's relentless innovation.

Other high-velocity companies demonstrate the pattern:
- Stripe built its empire on rapid iteration in payments infrastructure, shipping features and adapting to regulatory shifts faster than incumbents, processing trillions while staying profitable.
- Netflix runs thousands of experiments annually, making quick calls on content, UI, and algorithms—its culture of calculated speed turned streaming from niche to dominant.
- SpaceX and Tesla exemplify Musk-style velocity: rapid prototyping, failing forward, and pivoting based on real data, outpacing legacy players in aerospace and EVs.

The edge compounds because fast deciders learn faster. They test hypotheses in market time, not meeting time. In volatile 2026 environments—supply chain shocks, AI regulation, shifting consumer attention—slow decision-making is fatal.

Why Decision Velocity Is the Invisible Moat

- Time is asymmetric: A week faster on a key bet can mean first-mover advantage, locked-in customers, or avoided losses.
- Learning loops tighten: Quick decisions + quick feedback = exponential improvement.
- Talent magnet: High-performers gravitate to environments where ideas move fast, not languish in committees.
- Resilience in uncertainty: Velocity turns unknowns into data points sooner.

Without it, even strong products stagnate as competitors lap you.

How to Build a Decision Velocity Engine

Implement these systems to raise your organization's decision speed without sacrificing soundness.

1. Classify Decisions Ruthlessly
   Adopt Bezos's framework:
   - Type 1 (irreversible): Rare, high-stakes (e.g., major pivots, acquisitions, core IP sales). Deliberate process, pre-mortems mandatory.

- Type 2 (reversible): Most decisions (features, pricing tweaks, hires, marketing tests). Default to fast—decide in hours or days, not weeks.

Label every agenda item or proposal as Type 1 or 2 upfront. If it's Type 2 but dragging, force a 48-hour deadline.

2. Institute "Disagree and Commit" as Default Culture

From Amazon's leadership principles: Leaders must voice disagreement respectfully—even if uncomfortable—but once decided, fully commit (no sniping, no "I told you so").

Bezos used it personally: when his team pushed an Amazon Studios project he doubted, he wrote, "I disagree and commit and hope it becomes the most watched thing we've ever made." This saved massive time vs. endless persuasion.

In practice:

- Require explicit disagreement in meetings ("I'm at disagree—here's why").

- After decision: "Disagree and commit?" gets a verbal yes.

- Revisit only with new data, not lingering doubt.

3. Use Pre-Mortems for Type 1, Post-Mortems Lite for Type 2

- Pre-mortem (for big bets): Imagine the decision failed spectacularly six months from now. Work backward—what killed it? (Gary Klein's technique, used by McKinsey and Fortune 500s.) Surfaces risks early, reduces overconfidence.

- Post-mortem lite (for reversible moves): 10–15 minute review after action: What worked? What didn't? One key lesson? No blame, just data. Keeps loops tight without bureaucracy.

4. Set Velocity Metrics and Rituals

Track decision cycle time (time from proposal to committed action) for key categories. Aim to halve it quarterly.

Rituals:

- "70% rule" default: If you're at 70% confidence and info, decide unless Type 1.

- Daily/weekly "velocity huddles": 15 minutes to unblock fast decisions.

- "No-meeting decision sprints": Protected blocks for rapid calls on reversible items.

5. Leverage AI to Accelerate Without Losing Judgment

In 2026, use agentic AI for research, scenario modelling, and drafting options—cutting prep time dramatically. But keep human judgment for commitment. This hybrid raises velocity while preserving quality.

The Compounding Payoff

High-velocity organizations don't just react—they shape markets. They spot faint signals (from Chapter 1), constrain elegantly (Chapter 3), and act before consensus forms. In Sydney's fast-moving startup scene—fintech, AI, healthtech—this moat is especially potent against global giants.

Start today: Classify your next 10 decisions as Type 1 or 2. Introduce "disagree and commit" in your next team meeting. Run a pre-mortem on one upcoming bet.

Velocity isn't recklessness—it's disciplined speed. Build the engine, and the moat appears.

Chapter 5: The Second Product Is the Real Product

Your first product is rarely the one that builds an enduring company. It's the market research you get paid for—the expensive, public experiment that reveals what customers actually want, not what you assumed they wanted. The second product (or the significantly evolved version of the first) is usually the one that achieves true product-market fit, scales profitably, and becomes the foundation of lasting success.

This isn't a theory—it's a pattern repeated across iconic companies. The first version gets you traction, data, and survival. The second version gets shaped by real behaviour: usage patterns, complaints, adjacent pains, drop-off points, and unexpected "aha" moments. Founders who fall in love with their beautiful first child often stagnate or fail. Those who treat V1 as tuition and ruthlessly harvest learnings for V2 win big.

Classic examples abound:

- Instagram started as Burbn, a cluttered location-based check-in app with photos, plans, and more. Founders noticed users overwhelmingly loved and engaged with the photo-sharing + filters features. They killed everything else, refocused on photos, and re-launched as Instagram. That pivot (the "second product") exploded into a billion-dollar acquisition.
- Slack emerged from Glitch, a failed online game. The internal team chat tool built to coordinate game development became far more valuable than the game itself. They pivoted to productize that communication layer— turning an internal side tool into the core product that redefined workplace collaboration.
- Shopify began as Snowdevil, an online snowboard shop the founders built for themselves. Struggling with existing e-commerce tools, they created their own platform to sell snowboards. When they realized the real demand was for the platform (not the boards), they pivoted to e-commerce infrastructure—now a multi-billion-dollar empire.
- PayPal went through multiple iterations (from Palm Pilot IOUs to email payments focused on eBay power sellers), each building on learnings from the prior to refine the core value: fast, secure online transfers.
- Twitter (originally twttr) evolved from Odeo, a podcasting platform made obsolete by Apple's iTunes. The side microblogging experiment became the real product after podcasting failed.

Even in recent years, the pattern holds: many 2020s startups (e.g., those in AI tools or fintech) launch an MVP to test assumptions, gather usage data, then release a refined "second" version that narrows focus, adds killer features from user behaviour, and achieves escape velocity.

The graveyard is full of companies that never made it to the second product: they clung to the original vision, iterated incrementally without bold cuts, or chased growth before nailing fit.

Why the Second Product Matters More

- V1 is hypothesis-driven — built on assumptions, interviews, and guesses. It's often bloated or misaligned.
- V2 is behaviour-driven — shaped by actual metrics: what gets used repeatedly, what drives retention, what adjacent problems surface post-purchase.
- Product-market fit usually arrives on V2 — Marc Andreessen's famous definition ("being in a good market with a product people want") often clicks after real-world feedback refines the offering.
- Momentum compounds here — V2 benefits from existing users, brand, data, and revenue to fuel faster iteration.

Treating V1 as sacred delays the real breakthrough. Embracing it as disposable intelligence accelerates everything.

How to Engineer Your Second Product Success

Follow these steps to turn your first launch into fuel for the real winner.

1. Treat Launch as Intensive Market Research (Paid for by Customers)

From day one of V1, track obsessively:

- Which features get used most (and least)?

- Where do users drop off or churn?

- What support tickets or feedback reveal "adjacent pains" (problems your product doesn't solve but customers mention constantly)?

- What unexpected use cases emerge?

Set up dashboards (tying back to Chapter 1's signal metrics) focused on activation, retention cohorts, power-user behaviours, and qualitative signals.

2. Aim for the "Second Product Pivot" Window: 12–24 Months

Plan explicitly: Within 12–24 months post-launch, you will likely evolve or replace significant parts of V1.

- Gather data for 6–9 months.

- Run "kill experiments": Test removing features to see if engagement rises (often does—simplicity wins).

- Harvest "jobs to be done": Interview power users—what core job are they hiring your product for? Build V2 around that.

3. Ruthlessly Harvest and Prioritize

Use frameworks like:

- RICE scoring (Reach, Impact, Confidence, Effort) on new features/pivots, weighted heavily by real usage data.

- Adjacent pain matrix: List pains customers express → score by frequency + willingness to pay → build only the top 1–2.

- Feature graveyard: Maintain a public list of killed ideas/features—celebrate cuts as progress.

4. Reward Teams for Learning Over Shipping

Shift incentives:

- Bonus/equity tied to retention/usage improvements in V2, not just features shipped in V1.

- Publicly praise "kill wins" (e.g., "We removed X and churn dropped 15%—great learning!").

- Run "post-V1 retrospectives" focused on "What would we build if starting fresh with today's data?"

5. Protect Focus During Transition

- Use elegant constraints (Chapter 3): Limit V2 scope to 3–5 core improvements based on data.

- Communicate internally: "V1 got us here; V2 takes us to scale."

- If V2 is a full pivot, consider a "sunset plan" for V1 to migrate users gracefully.

The Sydney Angle: Local Relevance

In Australia's startup ecosystem—where capital is tighter than Silicon Valley and talent competes globally—nailing the second product is even more critical. Founders at companies like Canva (which iterated heavily from early design tools to the full platform we know) or Atlassian (evolving from plugins to enterprise suites) succeeded by listening aggressively to user data and boldly refining. Sydney's time-zone advantage for APAC testing means you can get faster real-world feedback loops—use them to accelerate your V2.

Action steps today:

- Review your current product's top 3 usage signals—what do they tell you about the "real" job customers hire it for?

- Schedule a 90-day "V2 planning sprint": Data harvest → pain prioritization → scoped roadmap.

- Commit: If data screams for big changes, make them—don't protect the first child.

The first product opens the door. The second product builds the house. Don't get stuck in the foyer.

Chapter 6: Talent Density Over Headcount

Hiring more people rarely solves problems—it often creates new ones. Adding bodies increases coordination overhead, dilutes focus, slows decisions, and lowers average performance over time. The real lever for outsized results is talent density: the concentration of exceptionally capable, high-performing people in your organization. A small team of A-players (top 10–20% performers) consistently outperforms a much larger group of average or even good contributors.

This principle gained prominence through Netflix, where co-founder Reed Hastings and former Chief Talent Officer Patty McCord built a culture explicitly around maximizing talent density. They prioritized hiring and retaining only "stunning" talent—people who could do the work of multiple average performers—over scaling headcount. Netflix famously implemented the "keeper test": managers regularly ask themselves, "If this person were to quit tomorrow, would I fight to keep them?" If the answer is no, the company parts ways generously (with severance and positive references) to make room for someone who raises the bar. This approach helped Netflix achieve extraordinary productivity (often cited as generating ~$3M revenue per employee, far above peers like Google or Disney) while staying lean and innovative.

Other companies echo the pattern:
- Bending Spoons (Italian tech firm behind apps like Evernote and Remini) focuses on "small talent, high talent density"—acquiring companies but integrating only top performers, keeping teams agile and output high despite rapid growth.
- Spotify uses its famous "squad" model: small, autonomous, highly skilled cross-functional teams that deliver faster and with greater innovation than traditional large departments.
- Broader trends in 2025–2026 show lean companies leveraging AI, automation, and global remote talent to build billion-dollar businesses with surprisingly small headcounts—proving that density, not size, drives scale in the post-industrial era.

The math is compelling: research and real-world data show that in knowledge/creative work, the best performers are often 5–10x more productive than average ones. A team of 10 A-players can out-execute a team of 50–100 B/C-players because they require less management, make fewer mistakes, innovate faster, and create positive peer pressure that elevates everyone.

Why Talent Density Compounds Faster Than Headcount

- Lower coordination tax: Fewer people mean fewer meetings, less communication overhead, quicker decisions (tying back to Chapter 4's velocity).
- Higher standards become the norm: A-players hire other A-players, reject mediocrity, and push cultural excellence.
- Better retention of top talent: Exceptional people want to work with other exceptional people—they stay longer in dense environments.
- Resilience to growth pains: Dense teams scale culture and output more easily; adding headcount too fast dilutes density and risks "talent decay."

Without density, companies bloat into slow, bureaucratic structures where average performance becomes the ceiling.

How to Build and Maintain High Talent Density

These steps are practical and proven—start with one to see immediate lift.

1. Define "A-Player" Clearly for Your Context

Avoid vague "top talent." Create role-specific criteria:

- What does exceptional look like here? (e.g., for engineers: ships 10x impact features with minimal bugs; for sales: consistently closes 3x quota while building pipeline).

- Use outcomes over inputs: impact, not hours or credentials.

- Benchmark: Would this person be top 20% at a peer company like Atlassian, Canva, or Stripe?

2. Implement the Keeper Test Quarterly

Borrow from Netflix: Every manager asks, "Would I fight hard to keep this person if they got an offer elsewhere?"

- Score privately (1–10).

- Top scorers: disproportionate rewards (equity bumps, promotions, public recognition).

- Mid/low scorers: honest feedback, coaching plan, or graceful exit (generous severance, strong references—no bridges burned).

- Do this every 90 days—it's not annual review theatre; it's a living density filter.

3. Pay Dramatically More for the Top 10%

To attract and retain A-players:

- Pay at or above top-of-market (Netflix pays high salaries, no bonuses—full value upfront).

- Use equity/phantom shares to align long-term.

- Accept smaller overall headcount: One $300k A-player often delivers more than three $100k B-players.

4. Hire Slowly, Fire Fast (But Humanely)

- Raise the bar in recruiting: Use work samples, reference deep-dives, and peer interviews.

- No "B/C hires" to fill seats—better a vacancy than dilution.

- When density slips: act decisively but kindly (e.g., Netflix's approach: generous packages, no shame in parting ways).

5. Protect Density with Systems

- Cap team sizes: Keep functional groups or squads at 5–12 people max.

- Run "talent audits": Quarterly review of density % (aim for 70–80% A-players).

- Celebrate density wins: Shout out when a hire raises the bar or a process cut reduces low-impact roles.

The Sydney Relevance

In Australia's startup and scale-up scene—Sydney's fintech, SaaS, and AI hubs like Canva (which grew with focused, high-calibre teams), Atlassian (emphasizing autonomy and excellence), or Afterpay—talent density is a survival edge. Global competition for top engineers, designers, and operators is fierce; paying premium for density and keeping teams lean lets local founders punch above their weight against US giants.

Action steps today:

- List your current team: Who would you fight to keep? Who raises the bar?

- Run a quick keeper test on 3–5 key people this week.

- Identify one role where replacing average with exceptional could 3–5x output—start recruiting for it.

Headcount is vanity. Talent density is sanity—and the path to extraordinary leverage.

Chapter 7: The Discipline of Boring Excellence

Flashy innovation wins headlines and pitch decks. Boring consistency wins markets, margins, and longevity.

The most enduring companies rarely look exciting day-to-day. They obsess over the mundane: perfecting invoicing, reducing support ticket resolution time by 12 seconds, shaving 0.4% off churn through tiny onboarding tweaks, documenting processes so new hires ramp in days instead of months. These "invisible wins" compound quietly while competitors chase viral features, celebrity endorsements, or the next hype cycle.

This is the discipline of boring excellence—the relentless pursuit of operational mastery in areas that feel unsexy but directly drive unit economics, customer love, and defensibility. In 2026, with AI automating creative and analytical work faster than ever, the companies that still win are those that have mastered the fundamentals no one wants to talk about.

Look at the evidence:

- Amazon didn't become the everything store by being the most innovative in flashy ways every quarter. It won through boring excellence: obsessive logistics (same-day delivery infrastructure built over decades), relentless cost discipline (working backwards from customer price points), and systems thinking (e.g., single-click ordering, Prime's compounding retention engine). Jeff Bezos repeatedly emphasized "working backwards from the customer" and measuring inputs that matter, not vanity outputs.
- Toyota built the world's most reliable car company not through revolutionary design every year, but through kaizen—the philosophy of continuous, incremental improvement in every tiny process. The result: legendary quality, lower defects, and margins competitors couldn't touch.
- Chick-fil-A dominates fast food not with revolutionary menu innovation, but with boring excellence in operations: obsessive training (employees memorize orders without screens), lightning-fast drive-thru times, spotless stores, and consistent hospitality—even when lines are long. These unsexy details create loyalty that outlasts trendier chains.
- In tech: Basecamp (formerly 37signals) has sustained profitability for decades with a tiny team by focusing on boring things—simple, reliable software; transparent pricing; no venture pressure; excellent documentation. They avoid the drama of hyper-growth and instead compound through consistency.

The pattern is clear: companies that prioritize boring excellence create space for bold bets later. Flashy companies often collapse under their own complexity, debt, or cultural exhaustion.

Why Boring Excellence Compounds

- It improves unit economics first — Lower costs, higher retention, better margins give you freedom to experiment.
- It builds antifragility — When markets tighten or competitors falter, your operations still run smoothly.
- It creates trust — Customers and employees notice consistency; it becomes your unspoken brand.
- It frees cognitive bandwidth — When the basics hum, leaders can focus on strategy and innovation instead of firefighting.

Without this discipline, even brilliant products erode under operational drag.

How to Cultivate Boring Excellence

Implement these habits—start small, measure quietly, celebrate invisibly.

1. Obsess Over Unit Economics Before Growth

Make gross margin, customer acquisition payback period, lifetime value to CAC ratio, and contribution margin your north stars—review them monthly before revenue headlines.

- Rule: No new growth channel gets scaled until payback < 12 months (ideally < 6 in SaaS).

- Celebrate when margins expand even 1–2% through boring fixes (e.g., better billing recovery, reduced failed payments).

2. Systematize the Unsexy

Build repeatable systems for:

- Onboarding (automated + human touchpoints that hit 80% activation in first week).

- Invoicing & collections (zero-touch where possible, gentle reminders that preserve relationships).

- Knowledge capture (internal wikis, Loom videos, Notion hubs so tribal knowledge doesn't vanish).

- Support SLAs (response time, resolution time tracked and improved quarterly).

Assign owners and review progress like product features.

3. Run "Invisible Win" Reviews

Every month, hold a short meeting (30 minutes max) focused only on:

- What small, unsexy improvement moved the needle last month? (e.g., reduced churn 0.8%, support tickets down 18%, ops cost per order down 4%).

- What one boring thing can we fix next?

No slides, no hype—just data and ownership. Publicly credit the people who made it happen.

4. Kill Drama, Reward Consistency

- Discourage heroics ("I stayed up all night fixing X")—instead reward preventing fires.

- Use "keeper test" (Chapter 6) to ensure people who excel at boring excellence are disproportionately rewarded.

- Avoid "all-hands fireworks" for big launches; save energy for steady compounding.

4.   Founder Modelling

As leader, visibly spend time on the mundane: review support tickets weekly, join ops standups, audit a random invoice run.

When the top behaves like boring excellence matters, the culture follows.

Sydney & Australian Context

In Australia's high-cost, talent-competitive market—where Sydney startups face global pressure but local operational realities (GST compliance, APAC time zones, supply chain quirks)—boring excellence is a massive edge. Companies like Canva didn't just design beautifully; they nailed boring things like seamless cross-device sync, reliable exports, and enterprise-grade security early. Atlassian built an empire on customer support obsessiveness and transparent roadmaps. Local founders who master operations can scale profitably without endless funding rounds.

Action steps today:
- Pick one unsexy area (e.g., onboarding, billing, knowledge base) and set one measurable boring goal for the next 30 days.
- Schedule your first "invisible win" review.
- Ask yourself: "What boring thing, if fixed forever, would free up the most energy for growth?"

Boring isn't boring when it compounds. It's the quietest path to extraordinary.

Chapter 8: Leverage Asymmetry – Hunting 1→100x Returns

Most people and businesses operate in a linear world: effort roughly equals reward. Work twice as hard, earn twice as much. Hire twice the team, grow twice the revenue. This linearity is comfortable and predictable—but it caps potential. The entrepreneurs and companies that achieve escape velocity hunt for asymmetric leverage: situations where a small input (time, money, code, relationship) produces massively outsized output (10x, 50x, even 100x returns).

This isn't luck; it's deliberate pattern recognition and positioning. Leverage asymmetry turns good businesses into legendary ones because the returns compound non-linearly. A single viral loop, one killer integration, one network effect tipping point, or one piece of evergreen IP can change the trajectory forever.

Classic and modern examples show the pattern clearly:

- WhatsApp → Acquired for $19 billion with only ~55 employees. The leverage came from network effects (each new user made the product exponentially more valuable) and a simple, lightweight codebase that scaled globally with minimal overhead.
- Instagram → Sold to Facebook for $1 billion with 13 employees after 18 months. Core leverage: photo-sharing + filters created viral distribution (users sharing = free marketing), combined with mobile-native design that rode the smartphone wave.
- Stripe → Reached multi-hundred-billion valuation with relatively lean teams by building developer-first infrastructure once (APIs, SDKs) that thousands of businesses then built upon—turning infrastructure into a platform with massive usage without proportional cost increase.
- Notion → Grew to unicorn status with a small team by creating an infinitely extensible workspace tool. One core product (block-based editing) enabled users to build their own systems (databases, wikis, CRMs), creating compounding value and organic distribution.
- In Australia: Canva leveraged asymmetric design—Melanie Perkins and team built a drag-and-drop tool that democratized design, riding the

content-creation boom and user-generated templates for viral growth, reaching billions in valuation with far fewer resources than traditional design software giants.

The common thread: find or create mechanisms where value creation scales disproportionately to input cost.

Types of Asymmetric Leverage to Hunt

1. Build Once, Sell (or Use) Forever

Digital products, templates, APIs, content libraries, AI models—create them once, distribute infinitely at near-zero marginal cost.

2. Network Effects & Viral Loops

Each new user makes the product better or more valuable for others (e.g., marketplaces, social tools, collaboration platforms). Design referral incentives or shareability from day one.

3. Platform & Ecosystem Leverage

Build infrastructure others build on top of (e.g., Stripe for payments, Shopify for stores, AWS for cloud). You capture value from their success.

4. Automation of Judgment (2026 Era)

Use AI agents to handle research, content generation, customer triage, or decision support—freeing human time for high-leverage creative/strategic work.

5. Personal & Relational Leverage

One great hire, one strategic partnership, one mentor introduction, or one viral creator shoutout can 10–100x reach or capability overnight.

How to Systematically Hunt Asymmetry

1. Run a Leverage Audit Quarterly

List your current activities, channels, hires, and investments. Score each:

- Input cost (time/money/effort) → low/medium/high

- Output potential → linear (1:1) or asymmetric (10x+)

- Current ROI evidence

Ruthlessly double down on anything scoring asymmetric; kill or deprioritize linear ones.

2. Ask the 1→100x Questions Constantly

Before starting anything new:

- If this works perfectly, how much bigger could the outcome be relative to effort?

- Does this create compounding (users bring users, data improves product, etc.)?

- Can this be automated or productized later?

If the answer isn't "potentially massive," reconsider.

3. Engineer Viral & Distribution Loops Early

- Build shareability into the product (one-click share, embed codes, referral rewards).
- Seed with power users who amplify (e.g., creators, influencers in your niche).
- Measure viral coefficient (k-factor): aim for >1.0 where each user brings >1 new user.

4. Create Evergreen Assets

- Invest in IP that appreciates: proprietary datasets, templates, brand content, open-source contributions that drive adoption.
- Example: Write once → blog post / course / tool that attracts inbound leads for years.

5. Partner for Multiplier Effect

- Seek integrations/partnerships where your product becomes the default in someone else's ecosystem (e.g., Zapier-style connections).
- One deal can unlock thousands of users you never acquire directly.

Sydney & 2026 Context

In Australia's ecosystem—strong in fintech, SaaS, edtech, and creative tools—leverage asymmetry is especially powerful because capital and team size are often constrained compared to Silicon Valley. Founders who master it (like Canva with user-generated design leverage or SafetyCulture with field-worker mobile-first tools) scale globally without proportional burn. With AI tools maturing rapidly in 2026, Sydney founders can now automate research, localization, and even early customer support at low cost—creating new leverage points unavailable even two years ago.

Action steps today:
- Run a quick leverage audit on your top 5 activities/channels—identify one to amplify and one to kill.
- Brainstorm: What one small change (feature, incentive, partnership) could create a viral or compounding loop?
- Set a 90-day goal: Launch or test one asymmetric experiment (e.g., referral program, AI-powered content engine, key integration).

Linear effort builds a business. Asymmetric leverage builds an empire. Hunt the non-linear edges relentlessly.

Chapter 9: Narrative Capital – Your Most Undervalued Asset

In business, tangible assets—revenue, IP, team, cash—get measured obsessively. But the most powerful, hardest-to-copy asset often goes untracked on balance sheets: narrative capital. This is the compelling, coherent story your company tells about itself—why it exists, why it matters, why only you can solve this problem the way you do, and where it's headed. Strong narrative capital shapes perception, attracts talent, justifies premium pricing, builds customer loyalty, and creates resilience during tough quarters.

Narrative isn't marketing fluff or spin. It's physics: a clear, authentic explanation of cause and effect that people (customers, employees, investors, partners) can repeat and believe. When narrative is weak or inconsistent, even great products struggle. When it's strong, mediocre quarters feel temporary, top talent joins at lower cash comp, and customers forgive occasional stumbles because they buy into the bigger arc.

Examples of narrative capital at work:

- Tesla → Elon Musk's master narrative: "Accelerating the world's transition to sustainable energy." Every product (cars, solar, batteries, autonomy) ladders up to that single, emotionally resonant story. It attracts mission-aligned talent, justifies sky-high valuations during loss-making years, and turns customers into evangelists.
- Patagonia → "We're in business to save our home planet." This isn't a tagline—it's the operating system. It justifies premium pricing, drives loyalty (customers repair instead of replace), attracts purpose-driven employees, and gives the company permission to sue the government or donate profits without alienating its base.
- Canva (Sydney-born) → From day one: "Empower everyone in the world to design anything and publish anywhere." Melanie Perkins repeated this physics-like story relentlessly—making design accessible, democratizing creativity. It attracted non-designer users, justified

freemium scaling, pulled in world-class talent, and created a moat through emotional connection that competitors (even Adobe) struggle to replicate.
- Atlassian → "Build with heart in a world obsessed with productivity." The narrative around collaboration, openness, and customer obsession helped them grow from plugin seller to enterprise giant while maintaining culture during hyper-growth.
- Apple (post-1997) → Steve Jobs reframed the company as "Think Different"—human-centered innovation against soulless corporate tech. That narrative revived Apple, justified premium pricing, and created a cult-like following.

In contrast, companies with weak or shifting narratives burn narrative capital fast: they chase trends, pivot publicly without explanation, or let mission drift. Perception erodes, talent leaves, pricing power weakens.

Why Narrative Capital Compounds

- Talent attraction & retention → People join (and stay) for stories that give meaning, not just salary.
- Pricing & margin power → When customers buy the story, they pay more and churn less.
- Resilience → Strong narrative survives bad news; weak narrative dies in good times.
- Distribution & virality → A clear story spreads organically—employees, customers, and media repeat it.

- Investor patience → VCs and public markets give runway when they believe the long arc.

In 2026's attention economy—short-form video, fragmented feeds, AI content floods—narrative capital is scarcer and more valuable than ever. The companies that own a crisp, repeatable story stand out.

How to Build and Protect Narrative Capital

1. Craft Your "Founding Physics" Story

Boil it down to one clear, cause-and-effect sentence:
- Problem → Why it must be solved (emotional + rational stakes)
- Your unique insight/approach → Why only you can do it this way
- Destination → Where the world is better because of you

Example (Canva-style): "Design tools are locked behind skill and expensive software → we believe everyone should create visually → so we built the world's simplest powerful design platform → so anyone can bring ideas to life."

Test it: Can your newest employee explain it in 30 seconds without slides?

2. Repeat It Internally First

Culture eats strategy. Embed the narrative in:
- All-hands openings
- Onboarding decks
- 1:1s

- Quarterly reviews

When employees own the story, they become walking billboards.

3. Use It Externally Sparingly but Powerfully

Don't spam it daily—save it for anchor moments:

- Fundraising decks

- Big launches

- Crisis communications

- Talent outreach

- Customer love emails

Consistency > frequency. One well-told story beats 100 inconsistent posts.

4. Defend Against Narrative Erosion

- Narrative audits quarterly: Does every major decision ladder up to the core story? Kill or reframe ones that don't.

- No mission drift without explanation: If you pivot, tell the updated physics story clearly.

- Guardrails: Avoid "we do everything" messaging—focus wins narrative battles.

4. Evolve Without Breaking

Narratives can mature (e.g., Tesla from "electric cars" $\rightarrow$ "sustainable energy ecosystem"), but the core physics should feel continuous. Communicate evolution as "deeper fulfillment of the original promise."

In Australia's ecosystem—where global perception can lag and talent competes with Silicon Valley—strong narrative capital levels the playing field. Local founders who master it (Canva, Atlassian, SafetyCulture) attract international talent and customers by owning a distinct, purpose-driven story. With AI flooding content in 2026, a human, authentic, consistent narrative becomes your moat against commoditized messaging.

Action steps today:
- Write your one-sentence founding physics story (problem → insight → destination).
- Share it in your next team meeting—ask for feedback on clarity and resonance.
- Identify one upcoming moment (launch, hire, investor update) to deploy it powerfully.

Narrative isn't decoration—it's structural capital. Build it deliberately, defend it fiercely, and watch it compound.

Chapter 10: Antifragile Cash Flow Design

Cash is not just king—it's oxygen. Run out, and the most brilliant strategy, product, or team dies instantly. Most business failures aren't caused by bad ideas or weak execution; they're caused by running out of cash at the exact moment when survival or scale was within reach. The secret isn't having *more* cash—it's designing cash flow to be antifragile: not merely resilient (surviving shocks), but actually strengthened by volatility, downturns, and uncertainty.

Nassim Taleb coined "antifragile" to describe systems that improve under stress. In business, antifragile cash flow means your financial engine doesn't just endure tough times—it uses them to gain advantage: buying cheap assets, hiring top talent on sale, acquiring competitors, or locking in long-term contracts while others panic.

Traditional cash management focuses on runway (months until zero). Antifragile design goes further: it builds multiple, uncorrelated cash engines, maintains buffers that grow in value during chaos, and turns volatility into opportunity.

Real examples of antifragile cash flow in action:

- Amazon (1997–2001 dot-com crash) → While peers burned cash on marketing and unprofitable growth, Amazon obsessively improved unit economics (lower fulfillment costs, higher margins over time). When the crash hit, it had enough cash to survive—and then aggressively invested in infrastructure (warehouses, tech) at fire-sale prices. The result: massive compounding advantage post-crash.
- Basecamp → For over 20 years, the company has run profitably with no outside funding. They maintain multiple small revenue streams (software

subscriptions, books, events, consulting) and deliberately keep burn near zero. Downturns barely register; they often gain market share as venture-backed competitors cut back.

- Berkshire Hathaway → Warren Buffett's empire is the textbook of antifragile cash: massive insurance float (customer premiums held before claims paid) generates low-cost capital that grows during volatility. In crises, Berkshire deploys billions when others can't or won't.

- In Australia: Afterpay (pre-acquisition) built antifragile elements by charging merchants per transaction (margin-positive from day one) while keeping consumer credit short-duration and low-risk. Economic uncertainty actually increased merchant adoption as they sought flexible payment options.

The pattern: companies with antifragile cash don't just survive volatility—they position themselves to win because of it.

Why Antifragile Cash Flow Matters in 2026

- Interest rates, AI disruption, regulatory shifts, and geopolitical events create frequent shocks.
- Venture funding windows open and close unpredictably.
- Talent and assets become available at discounts during uncertainty.
- Linear cash burn models collapse fast; antifragile ones accelerate.

How to Engineer Antifragile Cash Flow

Implement these layers progressively—start with the foundation and build upward.

1.   Build Multiple Cash Engines (Uncorrelated if Possible)

Never rely on one revenue stream. Aim for at least 3 engines that behave differently in downturns:

- Core recurring (subscriptions, SaaS, retainers) → stable but can slow.

- Transactional/high-margin (marketplace fees, one-time services) → can spike in uncertainty.

- Evergreen/passive (IP licensing, templates, affiliate revenue) → low-maintenance.

Rule: No single engine should account for >60% of cash inflow within 24 months.

2.   Maintain 12–18+ Months Runway – Even in Growth Mode

Treat runway as a strategic asset, not a minimum.

- Calculate true runway using conservative revenue assumptions (e.g., 20–30% below forecast).

- During good times, build cash reserves rather than maxing spend.

- In 2026: Use short-term government-backed facilities or revenue-based financing as buffers (not primary fuel).

3.   Design for Volatility Harvesting

Plan in advance what you'll do when others panic:

- Talent list: Top performers at risk during layoffs—have offers ready.

- Asset shopping list: Domains, competitors, equipment, ad inventory.

- Contract timing: Lock long-term supplier deals during booms; negotiate harder in busts.

- Marketing counter-cyclical: Increase spend when CPCs drop.

4. Protect Margins Ruthlessly in Good Times

- Avoid "growth at all costs" traps (subsidized acquisition, heavy discounts).

- Maintain gross margins >60–70% (SaaS benchmark) before aggressive scaling.

- Automate cost levers (AI for support, billing optimization) so margins expand under pressure.

4. Cash Flow Forecasting with Scenarios

Run monthly forecasts in three bands:

- Base case (expected)

- Stress case (-40% revenue, +30% costs)

- Opportunity case (what if we acquire X or double down on Y?)

Tie decisions to the stress case—live as if it's happening.

Sydney & Australian Context

In Australia's high-cost environment (salaries, compliance, taxes), antifragile cash is a survival superpower. Local startups often face longer funding cycles and currency volatility—making diversified engines and conservative runway essential. Companies like Canva (profitable early, multiple streams) and SafetyCulture (recurring + services) demonstrate how antifragile design lets Australian founders scale globally without constant dilution.

Action steps today:

- Map your current cash engines—identify the most fragile one and brainstorm a second stream.

- Calculate your real runway under stress assumptions.

- Create a 1-page "volatility playbook": 3–5 specific moves you'll make if revenue drops 30% next quarter.

Cash isn't the goal—it's the fuel. Design it to thrive in fire, not just avoid it.

Chapter 11: Decade Thinking – The Long Game Mindset

Most business advice is poisoned by short-termism. Quarterly targets, monthly metrics, daily hustle porn, viral growth hacks—all optimized for the next 90 days or the next funding round. They feel urgent, they look productive, but they rarely build anything that lasts.

The founders and companies that quietly dominate over decades think in 10-year increments. They ask: "Will this decision look intelligent in 2036?" They sacrifice short-term vanity (growth at all costs, headline-grabbing features, quick exits) for long-term positioning (brand strength,

compounding assets, deep customer relationships, antifragile operations).
Decade thinking isn't patience for its own sake—it's ruthless prioritization
of what compounds most powerfully over time.

Evidence from enduring winners:

- Amazon → Jeff Bezos famously told shareholders in 1997: "We will
continue to make investment decisions in light of long-term market
leadership considerations rather than short-term profitability
considerations." He accepted years of losses, massive capex on
warehouses and AWS, and public criticism—because he was building
infrastructure that would compound for decades. By 2026, AWS alone is
worth more than most companies ever achieve.
- Berkshire Hathaway → Warren Buffett and Charlie Munger have
operated on a multi-decade horizon since the 1960s. They buy businesses
with durable competitive advantages ("economic moats") and let
compounding do the work. No quarterly earnings calls, minimal PR, zero
obsession with stock price fluctuations—pure decade thinking.
- Costco → Low margins, membership model, relentless focus on value
and employee treatment. Wall Street frequently criticized it for "under-
earning" relative to peers. Yet Costco has delivered superior long-term
shareholder returns through consistent compounding of loyal members,
supplier relationships, and operational excellence.
- In Australia: CSL (biotech giant) has compounded for over a century by
investing heavily in R&D, plasma collection infrastructure, and global
scale—decisions that looked expensive or slow in the short term but

created unassailable advantages over decades. Atlassian similarly prioritised product quality and customer love over aggressive monetisation early on, building a foundation that supports sustained enterprise growth.

Short-term wins are easy and crowded. Decade thinking is rare because it requires saying no to shiny opportunities, tolerating temporary underperformance, and betting on invisible compounding.

 What Decade Thinking Looks Like in Practice

1. Apply the 10-Year Test to Every Major Decision
   Before committing:
   - Will this asset (brand, data, relationship, IP, system) appreciate or depreciate over 10 years?
   - Does this choice strengthen our moat in 2036 or just inflate next quarter's numbers?
   - If we succeed wildly here, does the world look meaningfully better in a decade because of it?
   If the answer is no on any, deprioritise or kill.

2. Build Assets That Appreciate Over Time
   Prioritise:
   - Brand → Trust and permission to charge more (Patagonia, Apple).
   - Data → Proprietary datasets that get more valuable with scale (Google, OpenAI).

- Relationships → Deep customer/supplier/partner ties that compound loyalty.

- IP & Systems → Code, processes, culture docs that improve efficiency forever.

- Talent culture → Density and loyalty that survive founders (Netflix, Atlassian).

3. Sacrifice Short-Term Vanity for Long-Term Positioning

Examples of deliberate trade-offs:

- Accept slower growth to protect margins and culture.

- Say no to big but misaligned deals or hires.

- Invest in infrastructure (R&D, ops, support) before it's "needed."

- Avoid excessive leverage or dilution that constrains future options.

4. Measure What Compounds (Not What Shines)

Track decade-relevant leading indicators:

- Customer lifetime value trend (not just this month's revenue)

- Net promoter score or relationship health over cohorts

- Talent retention velocity of top performers

- Margin expansion trajectory

- Brand perception studies or unaided awareness

Review these annually, not weekly.

5. Protect Against Short-Term Pressure

- If venture-backed: Set expectations early—choose investors who understand decade horizons.

- If bootstrapped/private: Use Basecamp-style transparency to resist external noise.

- Personal ritual: Annual "10-year letter" to yourself outlining where you want the business (and your life) to be in a decade—revisit it yearly.

Sydney & 2026 Relevance

Australia's ecosystem rewards decade thinkers more than most realise. Capital is scarcer, funding rounds slower, and global competition fiercer—making short-term burn strategies riskier. Founders who play the long game (CSL's century-long compounding, Atlassian's patient enterprise build, Canva's steady democratisation of design) often achieve global scale without endless dilution. In 2026, with AI accelerating change, decade thinkers position themselves to own the platforms, data, and trust layers that survive disruption waves.

Action steps today:
- Pick your next 3 major decisions (hire, feature, spend, partnership). Run each through the 10-year test.
- Write a rough 1-page "2036 vision" for your business—what must be true for it to be thriving then?
- Identify one short-term vanity metric you're chasing—replace its focus with a compounding alternative.

Short-term thinking is crowded and noisy. Decade thinking is quiet, lonely, and extraordinarily powerful. Choose the long game.

Chapter 12: Joy as Strategy – Sustainable Energy Wins

Burnout is not a badge of honour. It is a strategic failure.

The mythology of the exhausted founder—sleeping under the desk, 100-hour weeks, sacrificing health and relationships for the "hustle"—still lingers in startup culture. Yet the data and the lived experience of long-term winners tell the opposite story: sustainable joy and energy are competitive advantages, not nice-to-haves. Founders and teams that protect and cultivate genuine energy outperform those that run on adrenaline and caffeine until collapse.

Sustainable success requires sustainable human fuel. When people feel joy, purpose, and agency in their work, they think more creatively, persist longer through setbacks, make fewer costly mistakes, retain institutional knowledge, and attract other high-energy people. Miserable teams cannot build delightful products or enduring cultures. Joy is not the reward at the end of the tunnel—it is the fuel that keeps the engine running for decades.

Evidence from enduring high-performers:

- Basecamp has deliberately designed for calm, sane work since the early 2000s: 40-hour weeks, month-long sabbaticals every few years, no work emails after hours, profitable from day one. Result: 20+ years of consistent innovation with almost no turnover among core team.

- Patagonia structures joy into the system: on-site childcare, flexible time for activism/environmental causes, generous environmental grants for employees. Founder Yvon Chouinard has said the goal is "to make the best product, cause no unnecessary harm, and use business to inspire solutions to the environmental crisis"—a mission that energises rather than drains.

- Netflix (despite its famous high-performance culture) invests heavily in context over control: freedom + responsibility, no formal vacation policy (take what you need), top-of-market pay so people aren't stressed about money. High density of engaged, energised people drives output.

- In Australia: Atlassian has long emphasised "Build with heart" and practical joy signals—generous parental leave, mental health days, team offsites, and a culture that celebrates work-life integration. Canva similarly protects "maker time" and creative freedom, helping sustain energy through hyper-growth.

The pattern: companies that treat joy as strategy (not perk) compound human capital. Burnout cultures leak talent, creativity, and momentum.

Why Joy Is Strategic

- Cognitive performance peaks under positive emotion and adequate recovery (flow states, better problem-solving, lower error rates).

- Retention & density — Joyful environments retain A-players longer and attract more of them.

- Innovation velocity — Playful, low-fear cultures experiment more freely.

- Customer experience — Energy is contagious; happy teams create better products and service.

- Longevity — Decade thinkers (Chapter 11) need energy that lasts 10+ years, not 18-month sprints.

How to Engineer Joy as a Business System

Make joy deliberate, measurable, and non-negotiable—not an afterthought.

1. Protect Deep Work & Maker Time

  - Block 2–4 hour uninterrupted windows daily for creators (no meetings, no Slack).

  - Basecamp-style: calendar "quiet hours" or full no-meeting days.

  - Measure: Track "flow time" per person weekly—aim to increase it.

2. Align Work with Intrinsic Values

  - Regularly ask: "Does this project light people up or drain them?"

  - Give teams autonomy over how they solve problems (Netflix "context, not control").

  - Tie roles to personal purpose where possible (e.g., let support reps own customer success stories).

3. Build Recovery & Celebration Rhythms

   - Mandatory time off: Encourage real vacations (not just accrual).

   - Small, frequent wins: Celebrate invisible progress (Chapter 7) with shoutouts, micro-bonuses, or team lunches.

   - Energy check-ins: Anonymous quarterly pulse surveys ("On a scale of 1–10, how energised do you feel at work right now?") with action on trends.

4. Remove Energy Drains Proactively

   - Kill toxic processes, politics, or people quickly (keeper test from Chapter 6).

   - Simplify tools and comms—reduce notification overload.

   - Pay well enough that money stress isn't a silent killer.

5. Founder Energy as Leading Indicator

   - Model the behaviour: Take real breaks, protect your own deep work, admit when you're tired.

   - Track your personal joy/energy weekly—your state sets the ceiling for the organisation.

Sydney & 2026 Context

Australia's lifestyle culture (beach, outdoors, work-life balance expectations) gives local founders an edge—if they lean into it. Sydney teams that protect weekends, encourage surf breaks or family time, and avoid US-style burnout glorification retain talent longer in a competitive market. With AI handling rote work in 2026, human energy shifts toward creativity, strategy, and joy—the exact areas where sustainable cultures win.

Action steps today:

- Block 2 hours of uninterrupted deep work tomorrow—and defend it.
- Ask your team (or just 3 key people): "What part of your work gives you the most energy right now? What drains it most?"
- Pick one small joy experiment this quarter (no-meeting Friday afternoons, gratitude shoutouts, mandatory vacation usage).

Joy isn't soft—it's strategic fuel. Protect it, measure it, compound it. The businesses that last don't run on fumes—they run on fire that doesn't burn people out.

This completes the original 12-core secrets.
We now have the foundation solidly built.

Chapter 13: AI as Co-Founder – Integrating Intelligence Without Losing Control

In 2026, AI is no longer just a tool—it's increasingly treated as a virtual co-founder by savvy entrepreneurs. Solo founders and lean teams use custom AI agents (powered by models like advanced GPT variants, Claude, Gemini, or open-source alternatives) to fill executive roles: chief of staff, strategist, researcher, legal reviewer, marketer, or even "devil's advocate" advisor. This isn't science fiction—it's happening now, with real examples of founders running multi-million-dollar decisions or entire operations with AI "councils" of 10–15 specialized agents.

A defense-tech solo founder built "The Council": 15 custom GPTs handling chief-of-staff duties, legal checks, HR policies, finance modeling, and more—saving him ~20 hours/week. Other founders orchestrate AI as a virtual teammate for market research (hours instead of weeks), MVP prototyping (no large engineering team needed), GTM playbooks, and daily briefings. Tools like custom agents on platforms (e.g., ChatGPT custom GPTs, agent builders, or no-code orchestration layers) let one person simulate a small executive team.

The edge is massive for Sydney founders: Australia's high talent costs and competitive global market make AI leverage essential. A solo or 3-person team can now punch like a 15-person startup—compressing timelines, de-risking experiments, and scaling lean without premature burn.

But here's the critical secret: AI as co-founder amplifies you only if you retain final control. Over-reliance turns you into a passenger; thoughtful integration turns AI into an unfair accelerator while preserving your judgment, vision, and accountability.

Why AI as Co-Founder Works in 2026

- Compressed team size — One engineer + AI agents can ship what once required product, engineering, design, and ops.
- 24/7 leverage — Agents handle repetitive synthesis, scenario modeling, drafting, and triage without fatigue.
- Decision acceleration — AI surfaces trade-offs, runs simulations, and prepares options faster than humans.
- Cost asymmetry — Marginal cost near zero vs. hiring executives.

Yet pitfalls abound: hallucinations in high-stakes calls, loss of founder voice, over-automation of nuanced judgment, or "AI drift" where outputs lose alignment with core mission.

How to Integrate AI as Co-Founder Without Losing Control

Follow these battle-tested practices to keep humans in command.

1. Define Strict Roles & Boundaries
   Assign agents narrow, clear domains—like a real executive team:
   - Chief of Staff Agent: Tracks priorities, synthesizes daily inputs, prepares decision briefs.
   - Research/Strategist Agent: Runs market scans, competitor analysis, scenario modeling.
   - Devil's Advocate Agent: Challenges assumptions, flags risks.
   - Legal/Compliance Agent: Drafts reviews, flags red flags (never final sign-off).
   - Creative/Marketing Agent: Generates drafts, A/B ideas.

Rule: Agents propose, summarize, or iterate—you decide and commit. Use prompts like: "Act as my [role]. Provide options with pros/cons/risks. Do NOT make the final recommendation—flag where human judgment is required."

2. Human-in-the-Loop as Default Architecture

Build oversight into every high-leverage flow:

- Require explicit founder approval for anything affecting customers, money, brand, or strategy.

- Use "review gates": Agent outputs go to a shared dashboard/Slack/Loom for your sign-off.

- Implement probabilistic thresholds: If confidence <85–90% (many tools expose this), escalate to human.

- Track "override rate": If you override >30% of agent suggestions, retrain prompts or narrow scope.

3. Start Small, Pilot Ruthlessly

Begin with low-risk areas:

- Daily briefing agent (summarizes metrics, news, inbox).

- Research sprint agent (market validation in hours).

- Content/marketing drafts.

Measure ROI: time saved, quality lift, error rate. Scale only after 30–60 days of proven value. Use pilot frameworks: define success (e.g., "saves 10+ hours/week with <5% rework").

4. Maintain Founder Voice & Narrative Ownership

- Feed agents your core documents: founding physics story (Chapter 9), values, 10-year vision (Chapter 11).

- Use system prompts like: "Always align outputs to [your narrative]. Preserve [your tone/style]."

- Personally edit key external comms (investor updates, customer messages) to keep authenticity.

- Run quarterly "narrative audits": Do AI outputs still sound like you?

5. Guardrails & Continuous Refinement

- Data privacy: Use enterprise-grade tools (no feeding sensitive IP to public models without safeguards).

- Bias/hallucination checks: Cross-verify critical outputs (e.g., financial models) with manual review or multiple agents.

- Version control prompts: Treat prompts like code—track changes, A/B test versions.

- Energy check: Monitor if AI frees joy/energy (Chapter 12) or creates new cognitive load.

Sydney & 2026 Angle

In Australia's ecosystem—strong fintech, SaaS, healthtech—founders face talent scarcity and high costs. AI co-founders let you compete globally without massive early hires. Tools accessible via API (e.g., OpenAI, Anthropic, Grok integrations) or no-code builders let Sydney solos prototype fast, test APAC markets, and iterate before raising. With agentic workflows maturing rapidly, 2026 is the year lean Australian teams turn AI into unfair leverage—while keeping the human founder edge that defines enduring brands.

Action steps today:
- Build your first agent (e.g., "Daily Brief Agent"): Prompt it to summarize key metrics/news/inbox highlights.
- Define 3 roles you'd delegate first—start with one low-risk pilot.
- Set one boundary rule (e.g., "No customer-facing comms without my edit").

AI isn't replacing founders—it's multiplying the best ones. Treat it as a brilliant, tireless teammate. You stay the visionary, the decider, the soul. Control stays yours; leverage becomes exponential.

Chapter 14: Mastering the Attention Economy in 2026

In 2026, attention is the scarcest, most valuable resource on the planet—more than capital, talent, or even compute. Platforms, algorithms, and AI agents fight ruthlessly for every second of human focus. Feeds are engineered for addiction, short-form video dominates discovery, and AI-generated content floods every channel. The average person switches attention every few seconds; startups that don't master this reality get invisible fast.

The attention economy isn't new, but 2026 marks its maturity: algorithms reward depth + consistency over pure virality, owned channels (newsletters, communities, apps) outperform rented platforms, and short-form video remains the primary battlefield while long-form rebuilds trust. Winning isn't about going mega-viral once—it's about earning repeatable, compounding attention from the right people.

From current patterns:
- Short-form video (TikTok, Reels, Shorts, YouTube) still captures the lion's share of discovery, but pure virality is harder—algorithms now favor consistent creators who deliver value quickly.
- AI tools make content creation 10x faster, but also commoditize generic output—winning creators and brands stand out with authenticity, niche expertise, and human depth.
- High-performers build "owned attention" (email lists, communities, direct relationships) as moats against platform whims.
- Depth beats frequency: one high-value insight repurposed across formats outperforms 10 shallow posts.
- Personal brand and authority matter more than follower count—niche positioning + searchable expertise wins long-term.

For Sydney founders in fintech, SaaS, healthtech, or creative tools, attention mastery is a survival edge: global competition is fierce, but local authenticity + APAC relevance can cut through noise.

Why Attention Mastery Is a Core Business Skill in 2026

- Discovery is fragmented — No single platform owns attention; users bounce between TikTok, X, LinkedIn, YouTube, newsletters, and AI agents.
- Algorithms evolved — They now prioritize retention and value signals over raw engagement farming.
- AI saturation — Generic content drowns; human insight, storytelling, and trust win.
- Attention = revenue precursor — Strong attention unlocks pricing power, talent attraction, partnerships, and capital.

Without it, even great products starve.

How to Win the Attention Game Deliberately

Build a repeatable system—not chase trends.

1. Define Your Attention Flywheel
   Pick 1–2 primary platforms for discovery + 1–2 owned channels for retention.
   - Discovery: Short-form video (TikTok/Reels/Shorts) for reach; LinkedIn/X for B2B authority.
   - Owned: Newsletter/community (Substack, Beehiiv, Discord/Slack group) for compounding trust.
   Goal: Turn fleeting views into repeat visitors who buy, refer, or join.

2. Master Short-Form as Your Front Door

- Hook in 3 seconds: Question, bold visual, surprising stat—stop the scroll.

- Deliver value fast: Solve one micro-problem or share one insight in 15–60 seconds.

- Repurpose ruthlessly: Use AI tools (OpusClip, Descript, etc.) to turn long-form (podcasts, webinars, blogs) into dozens of shorts automatically.

- Consistency over perfection: 3–5 posts/week beats sporadic virals.

- Authenticity wins: Raw, real, Sydney-flavored content (local humor, APAC insights) outperforms polished ads.

3. Build Searchable Authority (Depth + Consistency)

- Position narrowly: Own a niche topic (e.g., "AI for Sydney fintech compliance" or "bootstrapped SaaS growth in APAC").

- Create pillar content: 1 long-form piece/month (blog, video, thread) → repurpose into shorts, carousels, emails.

- Use data/original frameworks: Share unique insights from your business—not generic motivation.

- Optimize for search: Keyword-rich titles/descriptions on YouTube/LinkedIn; build topical clusters.

4. Prioritize Owned Attention Channels

- Grow email list/community aggressively: Offer high-value lead magnets (templates, playbooks, Sydney startup guides).

- Nurture relentlessly: Weekly value emails, exclusive updates—turn attention into loyalty.

- Community flywheel: Let users co-create (AMA, user stories, challenges)—amplifies reach organically.

5. Leverage AI Without Losing Voice
   - Use AI for ideation, scripting drafts, clipping, captions, analytics—but human-edit everything public-facing.
   - Agent setup (from Chapter 13): Build an "Attention Agent" to scan trends, suggest hooks, analyze performance.
   - Avoid burnout: Batch creation (record 10 shorts in one session), automate distribution.

6. Measure What Matters
   - Leading: Watch time %, completion rate, save/share ratio (signals value).
   - Lagging: Owned audience growth (subscribers), conversion from attention $\rightarrow$ revenue/trials.
   - Weekly audit: Which content earned repeat attention? Double down.

Sydney & 2026 Edge

Australia's timezone advantage lets you test APAC trends early. Sydney's lifestyle + global outlook creates authentic hooks competitors can't fake. Local founders who blend niche expertise (e.g., regulatory navigation in APAC fintech) with short-form storytelling can capture attention faster than pure Silicon Valley plays.

Action steps today:

- Pick your 1 discovery + 1 owned channel.

- Create/test 3 short-form pieces this week: one insight from your business, repurposed.

- Build one lead magnet to start growing owned list.

Attention isn't infinite—it's earned. Master the economy of seconds, and the rest compounds.

Chapter 15: Hybrid & Remote Scaling Secrets – Beyond Zoom Fatigue

Hybrid and remote work aren't experiments anymore—they're the default operating model for most high-growth companies in 2026. In Australia, particularly Sydney's startup and scale-up scene, hybrid reigns supreme: surveys show ~55% of workers prefer hybrid (split between 1–2 or 3–4 office days), with employers increasingly offering it as a talent magnet. Fully remote remains niche, but flexibility is now "the new currency"— often outranking salary in employee priorities. Yet scaling hybrid/remote isn't about more Zoom calls or flexible Fridays; it's about designing systems that preserve culture, velocity, and joy while growing from 10 to 100+ people across time zones and locations.

The trap many fall into: treating remote as "office minus people in the room." This leads to Zoom fatigue, siloed teams, eroded trust, and talent drain. The winners treat hybrid/remote as a deliberate operating system—one that amplifies advantages (talent density from anywhere, focused deep work, cost efficiency) while mitigating downsides (connection loss, decision lag, inequality between office/remote).

From 2026 patterns: hybrid is stabilizing as the norm (often 2–3 office days for collaboration), with emphasis on outcomes over presence, AI-enhanced workflows, and intentional connection rituals. Aggressive return-to-office mandates exist in some sectors, but flexibility remains a deal-breaker for top talent—especially in Sydney, where lifestyle expectations (beach, family, outdoors) clash with full RTO.

Why Hybrid/Remote Scaling Is a Superpower When Done Right

- Talent access — Hire the best in Australia (or globally) without relocation. Sydney founders tap Brisbane, Melbourne, or regional talent.
- Productivity lift — Focused remote days for deep work; office for collaboration/innovation.
- Cost & resilience — Lower office footprint, geographic arbitrage (live cheaper while earning Sydney rates).
- Engagement edge — Gallup data shows hybrid/remote often boosts engagement/wellbeing—if managed intentionally.

But scale poorly, and you get disconnection, burnout, and "two-class" cultures (office insiders vs. Remote outsiders).

How to Scale Hybrid/Remote Without Losing Momentum

Implement these secrets to turn distributed work into a compounding advantage.

1. Design for Outcomes, Not Presence
Shift from "butts in seats" to clear, measurable results.
- Adopt OKRs or KPIs per role/team—review progress async via shared dashboards (Notion, ClickUp, or custom).
- Default to async communication: Loom videos, written updates, threaded Slack/Discord for non-urgent items.
- Office days = intentional collaboration (brainstorming, mentoring, social). Remote days = protected focus.
- Rule: No mandatory "all-hands" Zoom unless truly necessary—record and share for async viewing.

2. Create Intentional Connection Rituals
Combat isolation deliberately:
- Virtual watercooler — Weekly 15-min casual "coffee chats" (random pairing via Donut or similar).
- In-person anchors — Mandate 1–2 "anchor days" per week for co-location (e.g., Tue/Thu in Sydney office for key teams). Use for high-energy sessions.

- Team offsites — Quarterly 2–3 day gatherings (mix work + fun)—budget for them like product launches.

- Onboarding immersion — New hires spend first 1–2 weeks in-office (or fly in) to build relationships fast.

3. Build a Hybrid Playbook & Tools Stack

Document everything—no tribal knowledge.

- Playbook sections: Communication norms, meeting etiquette (default camera on, agendas shared 24h ahead), decision-making (async first), time-zone equity (rotate meeting times).

- Essential stack: Slack/Teams (async), Loom/Zoom (video), Notion/Confluence (knowledge), Linear/Jira (work tracking), Donut/15Five (connection/pulse).

- AI boost (2026): Use agents for meeting summaries, action extraction, or daily standup digests—freeing humans for high-value interaction.

4. Ensure Equity & Inclusion

Prevent "office privilege" bias:

- All decisions documented async—remote voices heard equally.

- Rotate leadership spotlights (remote person leads next all-hands).

- Measure engagement quarterly (anonymous pulses)—act on remote/office gaps.

- Career growth transparent: Promotions based on impact, not visibility.

5. Protect Energy & Prevent Burnout

- No-meeting blocks (e.g., Wednesday deep work).

- Encourage real boundaries (no after-hours Slack unless urgent).

- Mental health days + unlimited PTO (with usage encouraged).

- Founder modeling: Share when you're logging off or taking a surf break in Sydney—normalize balance.

Sydney-Specific Edge in 2026

Sydney's hybrid reality reflects lifestyle + economics: high earners and city dwellers dominate remote/flex options, while cost-of-living pushes geographic arbitrage (live in regional NSW/QLD while earning Sydney pay). Four-day weeks or compressed schedules are rising as the next frontier—potentially overtaking pure WFH debates. Local founders who lean into this (e.g., Atlassian-style autonomy, Canva's creative freedom) retain talent amid global competition.

Action steps today:
- Draft your hybrid playbook outline (start with 3 core norms).
- Schedule your next intentional connection ritual (virtual coffee or office anchor day).
- Run a quick pulse: "On a 1–10, how connected do you feel to the team right now?"—address gaps.

Hybrid/remote isn't about location—it's about intentional design. Scale it right, and you build a distributed powerhouse that attracts the best while preserving the magic that made you small and nimble.

Chapter 16: Building Defensible Brand in a Noisy World

In 2026, the digital landscape is a screaming arena: AI generates endless content at near-zero cost, short-form algorithms reward novelty over depth, and every feed is saturated with "slop"—generic, polished, forgettable output. Attention is fragmented, trust is scarce, and most brands blend into the background noise. The winners don't shout louder; they build defensible brand—a moat of clarity, authenticity, emotional resonance, and consistent authority that competitors can't replicate quickly or cheaply.

Defensible brand isn't about being the flashiest; it's about becoming the trusted signal in chaos. In an attention economy where AI agents increasingly filter choices for users, and consumers crave human depth amid commoditized content, strong brand becomes your unfair advantage: it earns loyalty, justifies premium pricing, attracts talent, and survives platform shifts or market turbulence.

From 2026 patterns:
- Clarity and consistency cut through AI noise (brands with a "strategic spine" of core identity outperform scattershot ones).

- Authentic authority (proven expertise over manufactured perfection) builds trust faster than slick ads.
- Emotional connection and values-led storytelling create belonging in fragmented audiences.
- Dynamic yet cohesive identity systems adapt across channels without losing recognizability.
- "Back to human" trends emphasize transparency, imperfection, and real stories over generic polish.

Australian examples shine here: Canva owns "democratizing design" with relentless simplicity, user empowerment, and visual consistency—turning a tool into an emotional ally for millions. Atlassian built "collaboration with heart" through transparent roadmaps, customer obsession, and a culture-first narrative that feels human even at enterprise scale. These brands don't chase every trend; they double down on a clear, defensible identity that compounds over years.

Why Defensible Brand Is the Moat in 2026

- AI commoditizes content — Generic output floods feeds; only distinct, human-rooted brands stand out.
- Trust is the currency — With misinformation and "slop" everywhere, brands that prove authenticity win preference.
- Attention = choice filter — Strong brand makes you the default or the remembered option.

- Resilience — Defensible brands weather downturns, platform changes, and competition better.

Without it, even great products get lost or copied.

 How to Build and Fortify a Defensible Brand

Follow these steps—practical for Sydney founders scaling in noisy global markets.

1.   Forge Your Strategic Spine (Core Identity)

Define a crisp, non-negotiable foundation:

- Why you exist (purpose beyond profit).

- Unique physics (your insight/approach no one else owns—tie to Chapter 9 narrative).

- Emotional promise (how you make people feel).

- Visual/voice guardrails (colors, tone, patterns that flex but stay recognizable).

Test: Can every team member explain it in 30 seconds? Use it as the filter for every decision, content piece, and hire.

2.   Prioritize Authentic Authority Over Perfection

Shift from polished ads to demonstrated expertise:

- Share behind-the-scenes thinking, failures, and real processes.

- Create original frameworks, data insights, or Sydney/APAC-specific perspectives competitors can't fake.

- Use "imperfect by design" (Canva's 2026 trend influence): embrace human quirks, raw storytelling over AI-smooth slop.

- Build thought leadership: consistent long-form (blogs, videos) + short repurposing for reach.

3. Engineer Emotional & Community Bonds

In a fragmented world, belonging beats broad appeal:

- Nurture niche communities (Discord, LinkedIn groups, events) where users co-own the brand.

- Deliver "treats" of joy or empowerment (Canva's templates, Atlassian's open culture).

- Use values-led guardrails: transparent decisions, decency in interactions—emerging as a quiet moat against rage-driven noise.

4. Create a Dynamic Identity System

Build for motion, not static logos:

- Flexible elements (patterns, motion, sonic cues) that adapt to platforms while feeling cohesive.

- Consistent across owned channels (newsletter, app, community) and discovery (short-form, LinkedIn).

- AI leverage: Use agents to generate variants, but human-review for soul.

5. Defend Ruthlessly

- Narrative audits quarterly: Does everything ladder to the spine? Kill drift.

- Guardrails for creators/partners: Clear direction + freedom (e.g., brand voice guides) so UGC feels aligned.

- Measure moat strength: Track unaided brand recall, NPS trend, pricing power, talent attraction speed.

- Avoid "platform everywhere" trap: Go deep on 2–3 channels that fit your audience (e.g., LinkedIn for B2B, TikTok/Reels for creative tools).

Sydney & 2026 Edge

In Australia's high-cost, global-facing ecosystem, defensible brand levels the field. Sydney founders face noise from US giants but win with local authenticity (APAC insights, lifestyle relevance) and "human-first" positioning. Canva's evolution from simple tool to productivity ecosystem shows how owning a clear emotional lane (empowerment, creativity) builds massive defensibility. Atlassian's transparent, values-driven approach proves enterprise-scale brands can feel approachable.

Action steps today:
- Write/refine your strategic spine (1-page doc: why, unique insight, emotional promise).
- Audit last month's content/decisions: How aligned with the spine?
- Launch one "authentic authority" piece this week (e.g., raw insight video or framework post).

In a world of noise, the defensible brand isn't the loudest—it's the clearest, most human, and most consistent. Build the moat deliberately, and attention follows.

Chapter 17: Regulatory & Sustainability Moats – Turning Compliance into Advantage

In 2026, regulation and sustainability are no longer just compliance checkboxes—they are becoming powerful, structural moats for companies that treat them strategically rather than reactively. Governments worldwide (including Australia) are accelerating ESG mandates, carbon pricing, supply-chain transparency rules, data privacy enforcement, and AI governance. Many founders see this as friction and cost. The smartest treat it as an unfair advantage: turning "must-do" obligations into proprietary strengths that competitors struggle to match.

Australia is a particularly interesting case. The country leads in several areas:
- Mandatory climate-related financial disclosures (aligned with ISSB standards) are now in force for large listed entities, with smaller ASX companies and large unlisted entities phasing in through 2027–2028.
- The Safeguard Mechanism caps emissions for the largest industrial polluters and tightens yearly.

- Modern Slavery Act reporting is maturing, with increasing scrutiny and civil penalty risk.
- The Treasury is consulting on sustainable finance taxonomy and greenwashing enforcement.
- APRA and ASIC are embedding climate risk into prudential and conduct frameworks.
- AI regulation is advancing (via the proposed AI regulatory framework and voluntary safety commitments).

Companies that move early and intelligently convert these pressures into durable edges: higher barriers to entry, pricing power, customer preference, talent attraction, capital access, and resilience against future tightening.

Real examples of regulatory/sustainability moats in action:

- CSL (Melbourne-based global biotech) → Invested early and heavily in ethical plasma collection, traceability, and sustainability reporting. This creates supply-chain defensibility (regulatory-approved sources are scarce), justifies premium pricing in plasma-derived therapies, and attracts mission-aligned talent and capital.
- AGL Energy (transitioning) → While legacy coal created headwinds, companies accelerating credible net-zero pathways (e.g., early movers in renewables + storage) are gaining investor and community support, lowering cost of capital, and positioning for future carbon-constrained markets.

- International players with Australian relevance → Patagonia and Unilever have long turned sustainability into brand moat; in regulated sectors (finance, superannuation), early ESG integration leaders enjoy lower risk ratings and stronger flows.
- Fintech & data-heavy startups → Those exceeding APP (Australian Privacy Principles) and building transparent, consent-first data models are winning trust in a post-privacy-scandal world—especially valuable in healthtech, fintech, and AI.

Why Regulatory & Sustainability Moats Compound

- Barrier to entry — Competitors face catch-up costs, delays, or reputational risk.
- Capital & talent magnet → ESG-focused funds, super funds, and purpose-driven talent prefer aligned companies.
- Pricing & loyalty power — Customers (especially B2B and younger consumers) pay premiums for verified sustainability/ethics.
- Future-proofing — Rules will tighten; leaders today become the standard tomorrow.

How to Turn Compliance into Competitive Advantage

1. Adopt "Regulatory Anticipation" Mindset
   - Track emerging rules 18–24 months ahead (e.g., via Treasury consultations, ASIC guidance, ISSB updates).

- Assign a "regulatory foresight" owner or small team that briefs leadership quarterly.

2. Build Proprietary Compliance Infrastructure

  - Invest in systems that exceed minimums and become hard to replicate: blockchain traceability for supply chains, audited carbon accounting, privacy-by-design architecture.

  - Turn data into moat: Rich, consented, high-quality datasets from ethical practices become valuable IP.

3. Productize Your Standards

  - Offer compliance-as-a-service features (e.g., built-in ESG reporting tools, audit-ready data exports, carbon calculators for customers).

  - License or white-label your frameworks to partners—creating ecosystem lock-in.

4. Integrate into Narrative & Brand

  - Weave genuine sustainability/regulatory leadership into your founding physics story (Chapter 9).

  - Be transparent about progress (including shortfalls)—authenticity builds trust faster than perfection claims.

  - Use third-party verification (Science Based Targets, B Corp, ISO standards) as credible signals.

5. Monetize the Moat

  - Charge premiums for "verified sustainable" lines.

- Access lower-cost green capital (sustainability-linked loans, green bonds).

- Win government contracts or preferred-supplier status that require high standards.

6. Measure & Communicate Moat Strength

- Track leading indicators: third-party audit scores, customer willingness-to-pay lift, talent application quality from purpose-driven candidates, cost-of-capital differential.

- Report publicly (annual sustainability report, TCFD/ISSB-aligned disclosures) to reinforce the moat externally.

Sydney & Australian 2026 Context

Sydney founders operate in one of the world's most ESG-aware capital markets (super funds manage ~$3.9 trillion and increasingly screen for sustainability). APAC supply chains face tightening scrutiny (modern slavery, deforestation rules). Early movers in healthtech (data ethics), fintech (responsible AI), cleantech (emissions transparency), and consumer brands (verified sustainability) can build moats that global competitors will envy. The window is open now—rules are phasing in, but standards are still being set.

Action steps today:
- Map your next 12–24 months of likely regulatory touchpoints (privacy, climate disclosure, AI safety, supply-chain ethics).

- Identify one area where exceeding the minimum could become a product/feature advantage.
- Draft a 1-page "regulatory moat hypothesis": What standard could we own that others will struggle to match?

Regulation and sustainability aren't burdens—they're the next frontier of defensibility. Move early, move authentically, and turn obligation into unfair, compounding advantage.

Chapter 18: The Quiet Power of Micro-Experiments

In a world obsessed with big bets, moonshots, and "disruption," the real compounding advantage often comes from the opposite: micro-experiments—small, low-risk, fast-cycle tests that cost almost nothing in time, money, or reputation but reveal high-signal information about what actually works.

Micro-experiments are the quiet engine behind most sustained outperformance. They let you probe assumptions, discover unexpected edges, iterate toward product-market fit, refine pricing, optimize messaging, and test operational tweaks without drama or boardroom battles. Because they are tiny, you can run dozens or hundreds per quarter—turning guesswork into data-driven certainty at speed.

This approach draws from lean startup roots but has evolved in 2026: AI accelerates hypothesis generation and analysis, no-code/low-code tools make execution trivial, and attention-economy dynamics reward rapid, evidence-based adaptation over grand launches.

Real-world patterns show the power:
- Amazon runs thousands of small experiments annually (pricing, UI tweaks, recommendation algorithms, delivery options). Many are invisible to customers; the winners compound quietly into billions.
- Netflix famously tests thumbnails, episode ordering, artwork, and recommendation logic at micro-scale before wider rollout—driving massive retention lifts.
- Canva (Sydney-born) iterated early features through constant small user tests: template variations, drag-and-drop behaviors, export options— refining simplicity and delight without blockbuster "launches."
- Atlassian uses micro-experiments in Jira/Confluence roadmaps: A/B test UI changes, workflow suggestions, and integration prompts on subsets of users before global release.
- Modern 2026 examples: AI-powered tools let solo founders test 50+ landing page variants in days; no-code platforms (Bubble, Webflow, Softr) enable micro-product experiments in hours.

The math is compelling: if you run 100 micro-experiments per year and only 10% succeed but each winner delivers 2–5× improvement in a key metric, the compounding effect is massive—far outpacing one or two "big swing" bets.

Why Micro-Experiments Compound Quietly but Powerfully

- Low downside — Failure costs pennies and hours, not millions.
- High learning velocity — Fast feedback loops tighten insight cycles.
- Reduces risk in big decisions — Validate assumptions before scaling.
- Builds antifragility — You thrive on uncertainty because you're constantly probing it.
- Fits lean teams — Ideal for Sydney startups where capital and runway are precious.

How to Build a Micro-Experiment Engine

Make this a repeatable system, not a one-off tactic.

1. Adopt the Micro-Experiment Mindset

Reframe every assumption as testable: pricing, onboarding copy, feature priority, email subject lines, support response tone, even internal rituals.

Rule: If you can't test it in <1 week with < $100 (or free AI/no-code), make it smaller.

2. Structure Every Experiment Simply

Use a lightweight template:
- Hypothesis — "If we [change X], then [metric Y] will improve by [Z]% because [reason]."
- Test size — 5–20% of traffic/users (or small cohort).

- Duration — 3–14 days max (longer risks noise).

- Success criteria — Clear before launch (e.g., +15% activation rate, p<0.05).

- Kill or scale decision — Pre-defined; no "let's see how it goes."

3. Prioritize High-Leverage Surfaces

Focus first on:

- Conversion funnels (landing pages, sign-up flows, pricing pages).

- Retention/activation (onboarding sequences, first-use experiences).

- Messaging (headlines, value props, email subjects).

- Unit economics levers (discounts, bundles, upsell timing).

- Internal ops (support scripts, meeting formats).

4. Leverage 2026 Tools for Speed

- No-code testing — VWO, Optimizely, or free Google Optimize alternatives for web; Typeform/Make for flows.

- AI acceleration — Use agents to generate 50 headline variants, predict winners, or analyze qualitative feedback.

- Analytics — Mixpanel, Amplitude, or PostHog for cohort tracking; GA4 for basics.

- Execution — Bubble/Webflow for micro-products; Zapier/Make for automations.

5. Run a Weekly/Micro-Experiment Rhythm

- Monday: Brainstorm + prioritize 3–5 hypotheses.

- Tuesday–Wednesday: Build & launch.

- Thursday–Friday: Monitor + decide.
- End-of-week retro: What learned? What to kill/scale/next?
Aim for 2–5 live at any time.

6. Celebrate Learning, Not Just Wins

Reward "great kills" as much as winners.

Maintain a public "experiment graveyard" + "winners wall" to normalize iteration.

Tie to culture: "We learn faster than we ship."

Sydney & 2026 Context

In Australia's ecosystem—where runway discipline is often sharper than Silicon Valley—micro-experiments are a survival superpower. Sydney founders face high customer acquisition costs and fierce global competition; small, fast tests let you validate APAC-specific assumptions (pricing sensitivity, mobile behavior, regulatory nuances) before burning cash on big bets. Canva's early obsession with user testing and Atlassian's iterative approach show how this quiet discipline scales into global dominance.

Action steps today:
- List 3 assumptions you're currently making about your business (e.g., "Customers prefer annual billing").
- Turn one into a micro-experiment hypothesis this week.

- Set up a simple tracking doc or Notion board for experiments—start running one by Friday.

Big bets get headlines. Micro-experiments get results. Run them relentlessly, quietly, and watch the compound curve bend upward.

Chapter 19: Founder Mental Models – Upgrading Your Operating System

Your mind is the operating system of your business. Every decision, hire, pivot, and crisis response runs through the same mental models—the lenses, frameworks, and default assumptions you use to interpret reality. Most founders never consciously upgrade this OS. They inherit default settings from early experiences, books they read once, or the loudest voices in their feed. The result: outdated heuristics that quietly limit growth, create blind spots, or amplify stress.

Elite founders treat mental models like software: they audit, refactor, and install better versions deliberately. A small number of high-leverage models—applied consistently—can $10\times$ decision quality, reduce emotional drag, and create compounding clarity over years.

In 2026, with AI accelerating change and attention fragmentation, upgrading your mental OS is no longer optional. The founders who thrive are those who run cleaner, more adaptive code in their heads.

Here are the most powerful, battle-tested models—many drawn from physics, systems thinking, biology, and history, adapted for modern business.

1. Inversion (Charlie Munger / Carl Jacobi)

Instead of asking "How do I succeed?" ask "How could this fail catastrophically?"

- Pre-mortems: Before every major decision, imagine it failed in 12 months—what killed it?

- Inversion checklist: What would guarantee mediocrity? (e.g., hiring average talent, chasing vanity metrics, ignoring unit economics). Avoid those first.

Benefit: Prevents disasters more reliably than chasing upside.

2. First Principles Thinking (Elon Musk / Aristotle)

Break problems down to fundamental truths, then reason up without analogy.

- Ask: What do we know is true? What can we never compromise?

- Example: Instead of "How do we compete with Canva?" ask "What is the irreducible job of design software?" → rebuild from physics of human creativity + computation.

Benefit: Escapes conventional traps and finds novel paths.

3. Second-Order Thinking (Howard Marks)

Look beyond immediate consequences to the consequences of consequences.

- "If we cut price 20% to win market share, what happens next?" (competitors match → margin war → quality erosion → talent exodus → death spiral).

- Use: Map decision trees with 2–3 layers deep before committing.

4. Antifragility (Nassim Taleb)

Build systems that gain from disorder (Chapter 10 cash flow is one expression).

- Seek convexity: small downside, unlimited upside.

- Expose yourself to beneficial stressors: micro-experiments (Chapter 18), voluntary discomfort (cold outreach, public commitments).

- Avoid fragility: over-optimization, single points of failure, debt that amplifies shocks.

5. Leverage Points in Systems (Donella Meadows)

Small changes at high-leverage points produce outsized results.

- Highest leverage: paradigms (core beliefs), goals, rules of the system.

- Example: Change incentive structure (ownership gravity – Chapter 2) → ripples through culture, decisions, output.

- Lowest leverage: constants, numbers, subsidies—don't waste energy there.

6. OODA Loop (John Boyd)

Observe → Orient → Decide → Act. Faster, better loops win in uncertain environments.

- Tighten your personal/business OODA: rapid signal capture (Chapter 1), mental model upgrades for faster orientation, quick reversible decisions (Chapter 4).

- In 2026: AI compresses Observe/Orient phases dramatically—use it to stay inside competitors' decision cycles.

7. Compounding (Einstein's "8th wonder")

Small, consistent improvements compound exponentially.

- Apply to everything: 1% better margins weekly, 1% better talent density quarterly, 1% clearer narrative monthly.

- Track "compound rate" on key inputs (talent, brand, cash flow velocity).

8. Opportunity Cost & Trade-Off Awareness

Every yes is a thousand nos.

- Ruthlessly ask: "What am I giving up to do this?"

- Use "hell yes or no" rule for new commitments (Derek Sivers).

- Protect founder time as scarcest resource—guard it like capital.

How to Upgrade Your Mental OS

1. Audit Current Models

Journal for one week: What default assumptions drove your decisions? Which felt outdated or emotional?

2. Install Deliberately

Pick 2–3 models above. Study one deeply each quarter (read primary sources, apply to real decisions, reflect weekly).

3. Create Decision Checklists

Build personal "if-then" rules:

- Before big spend: Inversion + second-order.

- Before hire: Talent density + opportunity cost.

- Before pivot: First principles + OODA speed.

4. Use AI as Mental Co-Processor

Feed agents your core models: "Apply inversion and second-order thinking to this decision." Use them to stress-test thinking without ego.

5. Review & Refactor Annually

End-of-year ritual: Which models served me? Which created blind spots? Upgrade the OS like software.

Sydney & 2026 Relevance

In Australia's ecosystem—where capital is disciplined, global competition is intense, and lifestyle balance matters—clean mental models are a force multiplier. Founders who run inversion + compounding + antifragility simultaneously make fewer catastrophic errors, compound quietly, and preserve energy for the long game. Atlassian's outcome-focused culture and Canva's obsessive user-first simplicity reflect upgraded OS thinking.

Action steps today:
- Pick one model (e.g., inversion) and apply it to your next 3 decisions this week.
- Write a 1-page "Founder OS v1.0" doc: list your current top 5 models + 3 you want to install.
- Schedule a 30-minute quarterly "mental model review" in your calendar.

Your business scales only as far as your mind allows. Upgrade the OS, and the hardware (team, product, capital) suddenly runs faster, smoother, and longer.

Chapter 20: Closing – Compounding the Unseen Edges – Your Personal 10-Year Playbook

You've now read twenty chapters. Each one is a current—a hidden force that, when swum in consistently, pulls you toward outcomes most people never reach. None are flashy secrets shouted on podcasts. They are quiet, stubborn disciplines: signal over noise, ownership gravity, elegant constraint, decision velocity, second-product focus, talent density, boring excellence, asymmetric leverage, narrative capital, antifragile cash, decade thinking, joy as fuel, AI as teammate, attention mastery, hybrid scaling, defensible brand, regulatory moats, micro-experiments, upgraded mental models.

Together they form something rare: a system for compounding unseen edges.

The difference between good and legendary isn't one big insight. It's twenty small refusals to do what everyone else does—followed by twenty small obsessions with what almost no one does. Over a decade, the gap isn't linear; it's geometric.

This final chapter is not more theory. It is your personal 10-year playbook: a simple, executable template you can adapt, print, revisit annually, and use to turn these currents into your operating reality.

Your 10-Year Playbook Template

1. Core Identity (Chapters 9 & 16)

- One-sentence founding physics (why this problem must be solved,
  why only we can, where the world is better):

____

____

- Emotional promise we make to every customer/employee:

____

____

- Non-negotiable brand spine (3–5 words/phrases):

____

____

2. Signal Dashboard – The 3–5 Metrics That Matter Most (Chapter 1)

1. _______________________________ (leading indicator)

2. _______________________________

3. _______________________________

4. _______________________________ (optional)

5. _______________________________ (optional)

Review cadence: Every Monday morning, 15 minutes.

3. Ownership Gravity Map (Chapter 2)

- People who already act like owners (top 5–10 names):

____

____

- Next ownership experiment (equity-like incentive, audit ritual, etc.):

____

____

- Quarterly keeper-test reminder: Set recurring calendar block.

4. Constraint Commitments (Chapter 3)

- Current one-metric-per-department rule:

____

____

- Next 90-day "no new initiatives" blackout period:

Dates: _________________ to _________________

- Anti-growth defense budget %: ______% of resources

5. Decision Velocity Engine (Chapter 4)

- Default rule for reversible decisions: Decide in ≤ _____ hours/days.

- Disagree-and-commit verbal check-in habit: Yes/No

- One Type-1 decision pre-mortem scheduled this quarter: Yes/No

6. Second-Product Horizon (Chapter 5)

- Current product version: V__

- Target second-product pivot window: _________________ (12–24 months from launch)

- Top 3 adjacent pains / usage signals being harvested right now:

  1. _________________________________

  2. _________________________________

  3. _________________________________

7. Talent Density Threshold (Chapter 6)

- Current A-player % estimate: ______%

- Target density floor: ≥ ______%

- Next keeper-test cycle: _________________ (date)

8. Boring Excellence Focus Areas (Chapter 7)

-   One unsexy system/process we are obsessing over this quarter:

____

____

-   Invisible win review cadence: Every _________________

9. Asymmetric Leverage Hunt (Chapter 8)

-   Current highest-leverage flywheel (network effect, platform, viral loop, etc.):

____

____

- One new 1→100x experiment launching this quarter:

____

____

10. Cash & Antifragility Buffer (Chapter 10)

- Current true runway (stress-case): _____ months

- Target minimum runway: _____–_____ months

- Volatility playbook moves (3–5 actions if revenue drops 30%):

1. ____

2. ____

3. ____

11. Decade Vision Snapshot – 2036 (Chapter 11)

- Where must the business be to feel like a decade win? (3–5 bullets)

____

____

____

____

____

____

- One short-term vanity we are sacrificing for long-term positioning this year:

____

____

12. Energy & Joy Safeguards (Chapter 12)

   - Protected deep-work blocks per week: _____ hours

   - Personal energy check cadence: _________________

   - One joy experiment running this quarter:

   ____

13–20 Integration Quick-Check

   - AI co-founder role active: Yes/No (which agent first?)

   - Primary attention channels locked in: _________________ +

____

   - Hybrid playbook version: _____ (last updated _____)

   - Regulatory/sustainability moat hypothesis:

   ____

   - Weekly micro-experiment target: _____ per week

   - Top 3 mental models installed and used most often:

     1. ________________________________

     2. ________________________________

     3. ________________________________

Final Instructions for you

1. Fill this template tonight — even roughly. It's your personal OS config file.

2. Print it or pin it digitally — somewhere you see it weekly.

3. Review & update annually — end of financial year (June/July) is perfect for Australia.

4. Add one current at a time — Pick the chapter that hurts most right now. Swim in it for 90 days. Then add the next.

5. Protect your energy — This playbook only works if you're still swimming in ten years.

The water is deep, the currents are subtle, but they are real. You don't need to chase the spotlight. You only need to keep choosing the unseen edges—quietly, relentlessly, for a decade.

Until then: swim well.